Poetry and Nature

A Symphony of Nature's Marvels:
Poetry Inspired by Nature's Wonders
and Mysteries

Sara Masih

India | USA | UK

*To my father, uncle and aunt for always
nurturing my passion for poetry.*

To my mother for always being there for me.

To my grandparents for their endless blessings.

*And to my sisters, for refining my poems with
their sharp critiques.*

*And immense gratitude to the Almighty: Thank
you for the strength to write and express.*

Acknowledgement

Thank you:

To J.K. Rowling, for igniting my love for writing—a hobby that blossomed into a lifelong passion. You will forever be a source of inspiration to me, and I assure you, I will always remain your admirer.

To the BookLeaf Publishing Team, for turning my dream into reality and bringing this book to life.

To my beloved family, for their unwavering support and constant presence, standing beside me every step of the way.

Preface

This collection of poems seeks to offer readers—especially kids and students my age— a way to understand life and nature through the lens of poetry. A language that is both profound and expressive, yet beautifully simple, poetry has the power to illuminate the world in ways that resonate deeply within us..

River

I am a river, ever-flowing,
I never stop, I never tire,
As pristine as the heavens above,
I carve my path through mighty mountains,
Flowing city to city, sharing my water,
After a long journey, I meet the ocean,
I am a river, forever in motion.

Ocean

I am vast and wide,
Blue as the sky,
Sometimes I am low,
And sometimes I rise high,
There are mysteries within me,
That you might never unravel,
Hidden in my steely depths,
A mighty Kraken,
Or a monster from Bermuda,
Whatever they may be,
They remain concealed within me.

Sky

Sometimes blue,
Sometimes gray,
Glowing fiercely in the heart of May,
Blue during the day,
Black during the night,
Sometimes sunny,
Sometimes cloudy,
Sometimes crystal-clear,
It's a battle,
to take over the sky.

Rainbows

Rainbows, rainbows,
In the sky,
Twinkling with all its might,
Shining after the rain is gone,
Looking lovely at dawn.
Bright and colorful,
A burst of hues
Igniting hope and happiness,
With its existence.

Star

Star so high,
in the sky,
shining so bright,
in the night,
with the moon in the light,
up in the sky so high,
Spreading all around the sky,
Like diamonds in the dark.

Flowers

Red flowers, blue flowers,
small flowers, big flowers,
white flowers, yellow flowers,
striped flowers, round flowers,
flowers, flowers, different flowers,
flowers of every kind,
orange flowers, pink flowers,
lovely flowers, smelly flowers,
green flowers, golden flowers,
spotty flowers, wet flowers,
flowers, flowers different flowers,
flowers of every kind.

Smile

Smile,
Smile for me,
Just stretch your mouth horizontally,
And the smile will appear,
Does it not feel good?
To wear a smile all the time?
Cause' I believe,
Sometimes, that's all we need to do.

Summer

Summer, summer,
Oh, lovely summer,
School has ended,
Freedom is here,
No exam pressure,
All left is leisure,
Summer is here.

My new friend

When I was all alone,
I didn't know what to do,
I wandered and roamed, aimlessly,
Until I stumbled upon the wonder of nature,

The trees danced and whispered softly to me,
the breeze covered me like a shawl,
the birds chirped and flew around,
and from that moment,
I realized I found a new friend.

Mysterious bird

You see a flying dash of colors,
it rushes past you and soaring up a tree,
then you hear a beautiful melody,
and search for the source,
you reach the tree and spot a bird,
but the most magical one you have ever seen.
She sees you and comes down,
and you frown,
as she has a little hurt,
you mend the cut,
and you become best friends forever.

Lion's

Hiding like a spy,
waiting for the right moment,
to pounce and attack.

Busy

Busy all day,
no time to drift and dream away,
working all the time,
it's just not fine.

No time to laugh or to play,
or happily begin the day,
too busy to notice anything,
like an ant working for winter,
what a life this is...

Poem's

I am ready,
with a bunch of poems,
some are short,
some are not,
some are good,
some are cute,
some are strange,
some are like a song,
my little bunch of poems.

Books

Read on, read on,
keep reading never stop,
all you need is a book,
to keep you company,
with a book you are never lonely.

Birds

Chirping all around us,
hoping, jumping, twittering,
living in harmony.

Life

There is life in a tree,
it says, "Come near me,"
there is life in plants,
most in the touch-me-not,
it says "touch me not"
there is life in you and all,
because you can breathe, sing, and dance.

Animals

Large and tiny animals,
Adorable and charming animals,
flying and walking animals,
extinct and living animals,
so many animals.

Mountains

Tall and snowy,
with sharp stones,
a pointed peak,
pointy as a thorn bush,
rocky edges,
a dangerous climb,
as dangerous as hiking through a ravine.

Art

An exotic blend of colors,
what a beautiful contrast,
a precise work of art,
crafted by masters,
there is meaning within,
hidden in the paint,
look from another angle,
and find out what it speaks.

Rain

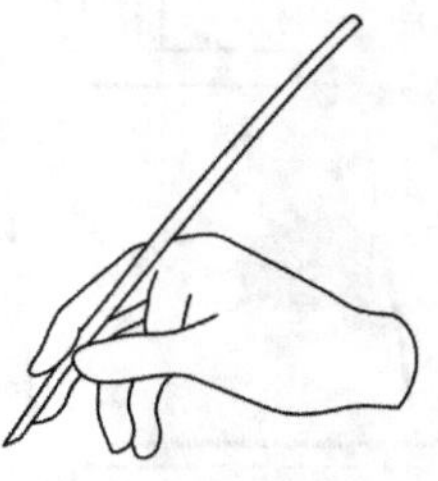

Drops falling from the sky,
the trees and plants,
look fresh and new,
mist is all around,
insects scurrying around,
for a new home,
the drops go pitter-patter,
rain is here.

Earth

Big and whole,
full of life,
water in oceans,
plants and life,
animals of all kinds,
birds flying,
fishes swimming,
The earth is brimming with life.

Poets

They work hard,
Day and night,
Writing poems they must compose,
Finding words and complex rhymes,
Just to fill the world with melodious chimes,
That have a meaning,
A hidden truth,
That's just what being a poet is.

Math

Full of numbers, full of shapes,
Patterns and equations,
For some, it is pleasant,
For others, it is jolly,
Mostly, it's holy,
But for me,
It's a tangle of numbers,
That is not at all jolly.

English

Words and sentences,
Sounding so alike,
And grammar,
With its comforting light,
Full to the brim,
With different meanings and different words,
Some are confusing as a blur,
What can you do?
It's the way of English.

Spring

Flowers blooming,
Butterfly's flying,
The end of winter,
Spring arrives,
Joy arises,
Trees are fresh and new,
Bears awaken from their slumber,
Spring is here.

Galaxy

Nebulas and stars in thousands,
Planets over planets,
Black holes swallowing sparkling comets,
Mysteries in a galaxy,
Galaxy's collide in a cosmic dance,
Creating new wonders,
In the vast expanse.

Dewdrop

Early in the morning,
Comes the dewdrop,
To refresh the plants,
For their daily routine.
Glistening in the soft light,
Whispering secrets of the night,
A tender kiss from nature's hand,
Reviving life across the land.

Dawn

The first ray of sunlight,
In the morning,
Not too bright,
Nor too feeble,
Just right,
A beautiful moment,
Of hope and joy,
Arrived at dawn.

Dark

Birds are returning to their homes,
With beaks filled with supper,
Bats are coming out,
To fly and glide around,
Stars are appearing in the sky,
To twinkle all night,
The moon is taking over,
Spreading its white light,
Because dark is here.

Sports

Running, falling, tumbling,
Into the soft ground,
Playing all around,
Soccer and football,
Basketball and volleyball,
Tennis and badminton,
What lovely sports they are,
Bringing joy and laughter,
Uniting hearts everywhere.

Sadness

Eyes are brimming with tears,
Tears rolling down your face,
An empty, strange feeling in your stomach,
Bothering you,
Feeling like you don't want to be you,
It's sad,
It's a heavy, suffocating sadness,
A cloud that refuses to lift,
A heart weighed down by invisible chains.

Friendship

Always have someone's back,
And they will have yours,
If you need someone to trust,
Or rely on,
Then you should know who,
Will stand by you,
It will always be,
Your truest friends.

Enemy

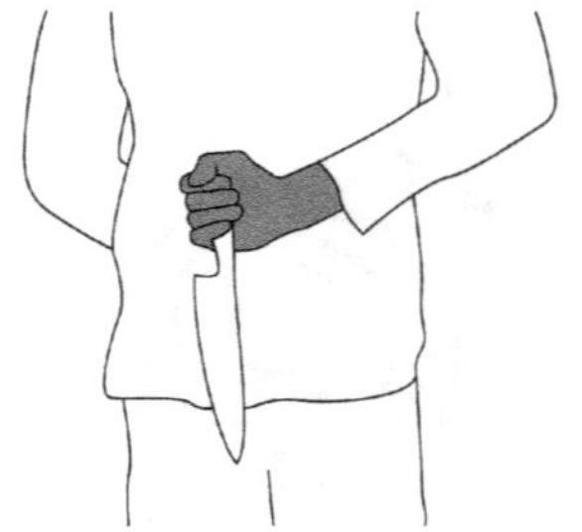

Someone whom you despise,
Hated with all your heart,
A person who ruined your life,
Causing endless strife.
Someone, anyone,
Who betrayed you,
Shattering your trust.
They are your greatest enemies, lurking in the
shadows,
Bringing pain and sorrow,
A constant reminder of betrayal.

Sunlight

Warm and soothing,
It gives a wild rush of hope,
Making you believe you can do it,
It energises you.

Science

Bubbling chemicals in the chemistry,
Biology is the study living beings,
And physics rules the scientific world,
With electricity and formulas.

Winter

Snow is falling from the sky,
Lakes are frozen, and rivers too,
Leaves are covered with snow.

Fire

Flames flickering,
Wood is burning,
Producing ash,
And smoke too,
A flaming red color,
Licking everything around you.

Autumn

Leaves are falling,
Turning, to shadesyellow, orange, red and brown,
Leaving branches bare,
Because autumn is here.

Parents

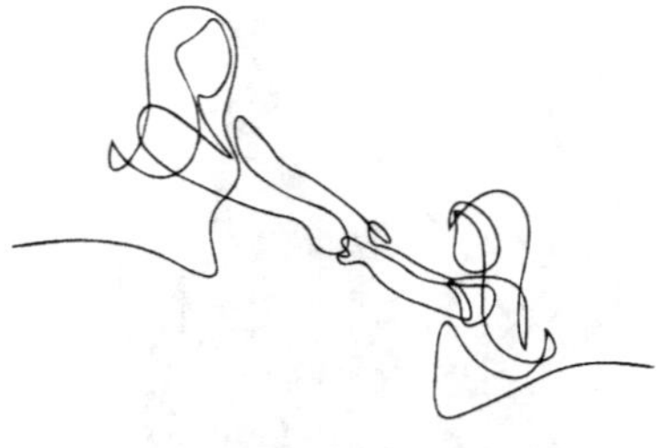

They care for you in childhood,
And guide you through your teens,
They teach you to be an adult,
And watch you grow up,
And leave them behind,
The least you can do,
Is help them,
And assist them,
Show them respect,
When they grow old like a turtle,
And wrinkly like a goat.

Bravery

Bravery comes,
Not from the body,
But from the soul,
Reveal your inner selves,
Confront your greatest fears,
That will be when,
You will be called brave,
Don't let your insecurities hold you back,
They are just a small step on the path of
bravery.

Birds

They may be big or small,
They spread their wings to fly,
To reach out to the sky,
They fly,
To search for shelter and food,
They do this to survive.

Sisters

They are naughty little ones,
Who cry their way out of trouble,
They are the people whom you hate the most,
But you should know,
Knowingly or unknowingly,
You would do anything for them,
Whether you want to or not.
Their innocent eyes and mischievous smiles,
Softening even the hardest hearts,
Binding you in a bond of love,
Unbreakable and timeless.

www.ingramcontent.com/pod-product-compliance
Lightning Source LLC
LaVergne TN
LVHW021303200726
843509LV00012B/1767